A COMIC HISTORY OF THE UNITED STATES

By

LIVINGSTON HOPKINS

American Fiction Reprint Series

BOOKS FOR LIBRARIES PRESS
FREEPORT, NEW YORK
1969

First published 1876
(Item #2765; Wright's AMERICAN FICTION 1876-1900)

Reprinted 1969 in American Fiction Reprint Series
from the printing of 1880

STANDARD BOOK NUMBER:
8369-7015-2

LIBRARY OF CONGRESS CATALOG CARD NUMBER:
77-85686

PRINTED IN THE UNITED STATES OF AMERICA

A COMIC HISTORY

OF THE

UNITED STATES.

BY

LIVINGSTON HOPKINS.

COPIOUSLY ILLUSTRATED BY THE AUTHOR FROM SKETCHES TAKEN AT A SAFE DISTANCE.

NEW YORK:
AMERICAN BOOK EXCHANGE,
TRIBUNE BUILDING.
1880.

LOOK OUT FOR PAINT

CONTENTS.

PREMONITORY SYMPTOMS.

The compilation of a history of any country is a serious matter, and should not be entered upon rashly. Before undertaking the present work, therefore, the author deliberated for twenty-nine years and six months, and then, having consulted the best legal as well as medical authorities, entered upon the task with fear and trembling. "Let me," he said to himself, "write the comic history of my native land, and I care not who makes the laws or the poetry." He hired a vacant lot on Nassau Street, and fenced it in, and there, surrounded by the paraphernalia of literature and art, he went to work with pen and pencil to jot down the leading incidents of American history to the best of a somewhat defective memory, and with all the enthusiasm of youth and a bilious temperament.

The illustrations have been our chief care, though the letterpress will be found equally reliable. It was our original plan to flavor these pages with a spice of romance, but after a prolonged altercation with Mr. Alden, our publisher, we decided to adhere strictly to facts. If the reader should happen to detect any slight anachronism in this work, or has reason to suspect that the unities have been lost sight of in a single instance, he will please notify us as early as possible.

When it first became noised abroad that we contemplated bringing out an illustrated history of the United States, we were deluged with letters from a host of well-disposed persons, such as Thomas Carlyle, James Parton, Wendell Phillips, and others of more or less literary ability, offering to "write up" to our pictures. Mr. Carlyle said he could do it nights. But the public was not to be trifled with, so we resolved to put our shoulder to the literary as well as the artistic wheel, as it were, and we flatter ourselves we have demonstrated in these pages that truth is more of a stranger than fiction.

CHAPTER I.

A FEW STUBBORN FACTS NOT WHOLLY UNCONNECTED WITH THE DISCOVERY OF AMERICA.

The sun was just sinking below the western horizon on the evening of September 11th, 1492, when a respectably dressed personage of sea-faring appearance might have been seen occupying an elevated position in the rigging of a Spanish ship, and gazing intently out over a vast expanse of salt water upon what at first sight appeared to be an apple dumpling of colossal proportions, but which, upon more careful inspection subsequently turned out to be a NEW WORLD.

We will not keep the reader longer in suspense; that sea-faring man was CHRISTOPHER COLUMBUS, and the object which attracted his attention was AMERICA!

This adventurous person had sailed from the port of Palos, in Spain, on the 3d of August with the avowed purpose of "seeing the world;" and who, thinking he might as well see a new world while he was about it, sailed in the direction of America.

For further particulars the reader is referred to the accompanying sketch, which, with startling fidelity, portrays the scene at the thrilling moment when a new continent bursts upon the bold navigator's vision. Pray cast your eye aloft and behold the great Christopher discovering America as hard as ever he can. The flashing eye,

EUREKA!

the dilating nostril, the heaving bosom, the trembling limbs, the thrilling nerves, the heroic pose, all vigorously set forth in a style which speaks volumes—nay, whole libraries for our artist's graphic power and knowledge of anatomy. We will next trouble the reader to let the eye wander off to the dim distance, where the new world looms majestically up, and stands out boldly against the setting sun, previously alluded to, which illuminates the scene with golden splendor, and bathes the new born continent in a flood of dazzling light.

If the patient reader will be good enough to examine this picture with a powerful microscope, he will discover, standing upon the utmost prominence of the new world, and in imminent danger of falling off, a citizen of the country who welcomes the stranger with uplifted tomahawk and a wild war-whoop.

Lifting our eyes skyward we see the American eagle soaring forth to meet the great discoverer, with outstretched pinions, and bringing his whole family with him. We confess that we, for one, cannot gaze upon this scene without envying Mr. Columbus the luxury of his emotions and wishing we knew where there was a new world lying about loose that we might go right off and discover it.

CHAPTER II.

IN WHICH THE EARLY LIFE OF THIS MAN COLUMBUS IS INQUIRED INTO—DISAPPOINTED PARENTS—THE BANE OF GENIUS—"POOH-POOH!"—CONVINCING ARGUMENTS.

Christopher Columbus was born at Genoa in Italy, a country chiefly famous for its talented organ-grinders. The youthful Christopher soon made the melancholy discovery that he had no talent in that direction. His tastes the rather took a scientific turn. This was a sad blow to his fond parents, who *did* hope their son would take a turn at the hurdy-gurdy instead.

His aged father pointed out that Science

was low and unprofitable, Geology was a humbug, Meteorology and Madness were synonymous terms, and Astronomy ought to be spelled with two S's.

In vain his doting mother gently sought to woo him to loftier aims, and, in the fondness of a mother's love, even presented him with a toy barrel-organ which played three bars of "Turn, sinner, turn," in the hope that it might change the whole current of his life; but the undutiful child immediately traded it off to another boy for a bamboo fishing rod, out of which he constructed a telescope, and he used to lie upon his back for hours, far, far into the night, catching cold and scouring the heavens with this crude invention. One night his sorrow-stricken parents found him thus, and they knew from that moment that all was lost!

EARLY AQUATIC TENDENCIES EVINCED BY COLUMBUS.

Our hero took to the water naturally very early in life. Let the youth of America remember this. Let the youth of every land who contemplate discovering new worlds remember that strong drink is fatal to the discovery business; for it is our candid opinion, that, had Christopher Columbus taken to, say strong coffee in his very earliest infancy, the chances are that America would never have had a Centennial, and these pages had never been written. Two circumstances which the stoutest heart among us cannot for a moment contemplate without a shudder.

When Columbus reached man's estate he became a hard student, and spent the most of his time in his library,

> "Reading books that never mortal
> Ever dared to read before."

COLUMBUS AMONG HIS BOOKS.

His mind, consequently, soared beyond the pale of mere existing facts and circumstances, and sought to fold its eager pinions on lofty roosting places yet undiscovered.

And thus it was, that, after revolving the matter in his mind for forty years or more, Columbus arrived at the conclusion that the earth was round, not flat, (as was the popular belief at that time,) and boldly said so in round terms. People called him a lunatic, an original character, and other harsh names, and otherwise pooh-pooh'd the idea.

But Columbus not only adhered to his theory, but went so far as to assert that by sailing due west from Europe you would, if you kept on sailing, bring up somewhere in eastern Asia.

"Oh, come now, Christopher! really, this

LOOK OUT FOR PAINT!
PHILADELPHIA
Columbus and Queen Isabella

is going to far!" is what public opinion said, and when our hero petitioned the Italian Congress to fit out an expedition and let him prove his theory, it magnanimously offered to set him up in business with a first-class barrel-organ and an educated monkey cashier on condition of his leaving the country once for all; but Columbus, expressing his regret for his lack of musical ability, declined this generous offer and turned with a sigh to other governments for assistance. Finally, after fifteen years of effort, he succeeded in convincing Queen Isabella of Spain that there was an undiscovered country beyond the seas, overflowing with milk and honey, which it would be worth while to "work up." He proved his theory with the aid of an egg, (which he made stand on end,) an old Boston City Directory, and a ground plan of Philadelphia, (see school books,) and demonstrated to the good lady's entire satisfaction that she might realize largely by fitting out an expedition and let him at its head go and discover it.

So conclusive were these arguments to the mind of Queen Isabella that the good old soul allowed him to fit out an expedition at his own expense, and gave him *carte blanche* to discover America as much as he wanted to. We have seen how well he succeeded. All this took place three hundred and eighty-three years, four months, and five days ago, but it seems to us but yesterday.

Ah! how time flies!

CHAPTER III.

TREATS OF OTHER DISCOVERIES AND DOES GREAT CREDIT TO THE AUTHOR'S SENSE OF JUSTICE.

On the return of Columbus to Spain, he published a map of his voyage in one of the illustrated papers of the day. Through the courtesy of the publishers of that paper we are enabled to place this map before our readers.

Here it is translated from the original Spanish. If the gentle reader can make head or tail of it he is more gentle even than we had at first supposed. The publication of this map at the time naturally inspired others with the spirit of adventure, and.

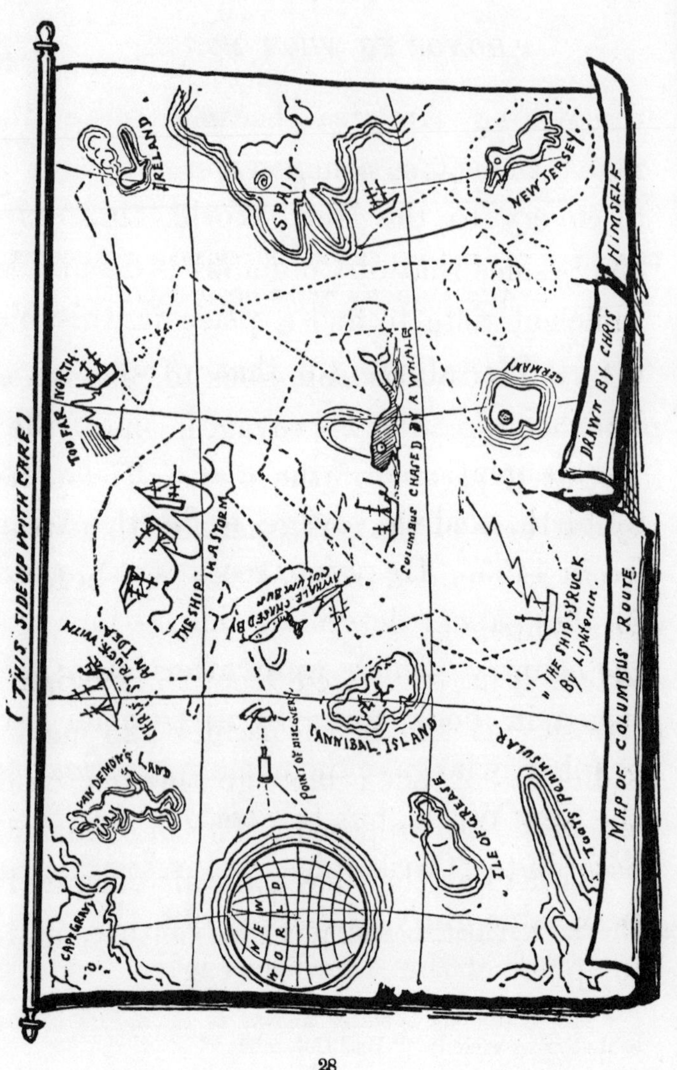
(THIS SIDE UP WITH CARE)
MAP OF COLUMBUS' ROUTE.
DRAWN BY CHRIS HIMSELF
IRELAND
SPAIN
NEW JERSEY
GERMANY
TOO FAR NORTH.
COLUMBUS CHASED BY A WHALE
THE SHIP IN A STORM
A WHALE CHASED BY COLUMBUS
" THE SHIP STRUCK BY LIGHTNIN.
CHRIS STRUCK WITH AN IDEA.
CANNIBAL ISLAND
POINT OF DISCOVERY
VAN DEMON'S LAND
NEW WORLD
CAPE GRAVY
" ISLE OF GREASE
TOOTS' PENINSULAR

discovering America became quite the rage. Indeed, so common were voyages of discovery to the New World, that only one besides that of Columbus is deemed of sufficient note to find a place in this history. We allude to that of Americus Vespucius.

This gentleman, who was a Florentine by birth, made a voyage to South America in 1499. He wrote sensational letters to the papers describing his voyage and the country, which were afterwards published in book form by a German geographer, who gave the name "America" to the New World, but this history cheerfully accords to *Christopher Columbus the imperishable glory of finding out the roosting-place of the American eagle.

* Mr. Columbus is better known as the author of that soul-stirring melody, "Hail Columbia!"

CHAPTER IV.

HAVING TO HIS ENTIRE SATISFACTION SETTLED THE QUESTION AS TO WHO DISCOVERED AMERICA, THE AUTHOR PROCEEDS TO SETTLE THE COUNTRY ITSELF—JOHN SMITH IS MENTIONED—JOHN SMITH ON THE ROSTRUM—JOHN SMITH IN DIFFICULTIES—THE PLOT THICKENS AS FAR AS J. SMITH IS CONCERNED—THE DEATH PENALTY—SLOW MUSIC—* * * * SAVED!

It was a century or more after the events narrated in the last chapter before any attempt was made to establish a colony in America, or before civilization got any permanent foothold.

In 1606 a certain "London company" got out a patent on Virginia, and the next year sent over a ship-load of old bachelors

to settle its claim. They landed at Jamestown in the month of May, and here the wretched outcasts went into lodgings for single gentlemen.

The whole country was a howling wilderness, overrun with Indians, wild beasts and Jersey mosquitoes.

These hardy pioneers had come to an unexplored region with a vague, general idea that they were to dig gold, trade with the Indians, get enormously rich and return home. So sanguine were they of speedy success that they planted nothing that year. The few sandwiches they had brought with them were soon consumed, the gold did not "pan out," the Indians drove very hard bargains, offering a ready market for hair, but giving little or nothing in return.

A BUSINESS TRANSACTION.

To make matters worse, the Fevernager, a terrible disease of the period, got among them, and by fall only a handful of the colonists remained, and these were a very shaky lot indeed, with not clothing enough among them to wad a shot-gun.

Among this seedy band was one John Smith, who, being out of funds himself, and a public spirited person withal, saw that unless provisions could be obtained shortly, the scheme of colonizing America would be a failure.

He went into the lecture field, holding forth to large and fashionable audiences, composed of intelligent savages, upon the science of navigation, illustrating his lecture with an old mariner's compass that indicated all four of the cardinal points at once, and a superannuated bulls-eye watch that

John Smith on the Rostrum.

would do nothing but tick. These simple-minded children of nature listened with attentive ears, and looked on with wondering eyes, and came down largely with green corn, sardines, silk hats, hard boiled eggs, fall overcoats, pickled oysters, red handkerchiefs, ice cream, dried herring, kid gloves, pickled tripe, and other Indian luxuries, which proved invaluable to the starving, threadbare colonists. Thus it is seen that Mr. Smith obtained on *tick** what he had no cash to pay for.

Although Mr. Smith was regarded as a talented man from a scientific point of view, and was even mentioned in the native papers as undoubtedly a god, yet he was sometimes grossly misunderstood by these

---

* The reader may occasionally find this sort of thing in these pages but he is entreated not to be startled.

artless aborigines, and on one occasion they arrested him on a general charge of hocus-pocus or witchcraft, and carried him before Chief Justice Powhatan to be tried for his life.

The jury brought in a verdict of "guilty" on all the counts, and the hapless Smith was condemned to death. His counsel did all they could to establish an alibi, but in vain. It was a clear case; a fair trial had been given their pale brother and he must suffer the penalty. As a last resort, Mr. Smith offered, first, his bull's-eye watch, and finally, the old mariner's compass, for his life, but Judge Powhatan could not see the point. He had never seen a white man die, and was panting for a new sensation. He therefore ordered the entertainment to proceed without more delay.

Having previously had his scalp removed, the doomed man thanked his captors for all their kindness, and requesting the executioner to make a good job of it, placed his head upon the fatal block. The dread instrument of death was uplifted, and Mr. Smith was really apprehensive that his time had come. He closed his eyes and whistled the plaintive air,

"Who will care for my mother-in-law now?"

There was a hush of pleasant anticipation—a deadly silence—you might have heard a pin drop—indeed, you might have heard ten pins drop.

* * * * * * *

At this supreme moment Pocahontas, the beautiful and accomplished daughter of Judge Powhatan, appeared upon the scene, tastefully dressed as a ballet girl, and using

POCAHONTAS SAVING THE LIFE OF CAPTAIN SMITH

some pretty strong arguments with her father, obtained from him a stay of proceedings, and the prisoner's life was spared.

Powhatan apologized to Mr. Smith for the loss of his hair, and handsomely offered to buy him a wig. John admitted that it was rather a closer shave than he had been accustomed to, but at the same time he begged the learned gentleman not to mention it, and made the best of his way back to Jamestown laden with presents, which were subsequently stolen by the donors.

Many persons look upon this incident as apocryphal, but we are prepared to assure them upon personal knowledge of its truthfulness. For, during a brief but bloodless campaign in Virginia in 1864, whither we had gone as a gory "hundred day's man" to put down the Rebellion, sixteen different identical spots were pointed out to us where Pocahontas saved the life of Captain Smith.

If there be any lingering doubt in the mind of any one we point him in triumph to any of our ably written city directories, the careful perusal of which will convince the most sceptical mind of Mr. Smith's safety.

Pocahontas afterwards married a young English lord, (our American girls marry titles whenever they get the chance,) and at last accounts was doing very well.

Mr. Smith was elected president, by a large majority, of the little colony, which began to thrive henceforth, and was soon reinforced by other adventurers from England.

In the fall of 1609 Mr. Smith was com-

GREAT SEAL OF VIRGINIA—
SKETCHED ON THE SPOT.

pelled to return to England on account of a boil on his neck, or to have a tooth drawn, we forget which—but that is a mere detail.

Virginia became a fixed fact, and in 1664 was ceded to the Crown of Great Britain, which maintained jurisdiction over it until about the year 1776. On page 42 we reproduce the great Seal of Virginia. The allegory is so strikingly and beautifully obvious as to need no further elucidation.

CHAPTER V.

TREATS OF THE EARLY HISTORY OF MASSACHUSETTS AND MAKES MENTION OF A PILGRIM FATHER OR TWO, ALSO SHOWS WHAT A GOOD MEMORY THE AUTHOR HAS FOR DATES.

Massachusetts was first settled by Pilgrim Fathers who sailed from England in the year 1620 on board the *May Flour*, giving directions to the captain to set them down at some place where they could enjoy religious freedom, trusting rather to his knowledge of Navigation than of Theology to land them at the right place.

Thinking wild savages least likely to entertain pronounced religious prejudices, the captain of the *May Flour* bethought

MAYFLOWER
LANDING OF THE PILGRIMS

him of America, and landed them hap-hazard at Plymouth, Massachusetts, on the 21st of December, 1620. The Pilgrims made themselves as comfortable on Plymouth Rock as possible, and formed a treaty with the Indians which lasted several days.

The accompanying sketch not only accurately illustrates the event just narrated, but gives us a faithful and striking portrait of each of the Pilgrim Fathers, which will be immediately recognized by all their acquaintances. The drawing is made from a photograph taken on the spot by an artistic Pilgrim, who brought his camera with him, hoping to turn a penny by photographing the natives. We may here incidentally remark that his first native "subject," dissatisfied with the result of a "sitting," scalped the artist and confiscated

THE PILGRIM FATHERS
CONVERTING A QUAKER

his camera, which he converted into a rude sort of accordion. This instrument was the cause in a remote way of the ingenious native's death, for he was promptly assassinated by his indignant neighbors. Let the young man over the way, who has recently traded his mother's flat-irons for a concertina, take warning.

As some of our readers may not know what a Pilgrim Father is, and as it is the business of this book to make straight all the crooked paths of history, we beg to state that a Pilgrim Father is a fellow who believes in *hard-money* piety, if we may be allowed the expression, and with whom no paper substitute will pass current. All others are counterfeit, and none genuine without the signature, "Puritan."

Having come so far to enjoy religious

freedom, the Puritans took it unkind if any one ventured to differ with them. Our illustration shows their style of reforming Quakers in 1656. They used, as will be seen, a very irresistible line of argument, and the dissenting party thus "dealt" with generally found it useless to combat old-established prejudices.

It is not for the unimpassioned historian to comment upon such a system of orthodoxy. We will say, however, that the Puritans *meant* well, and were on the whole worthy sort of persons. At any rate, Plymouth Rock was a success, and may be seen to this day (with certain modifications) in the identical spot where the Pilgrim Fathers found it.

CHAPTER VI

CONNECTICUT—INDIAN DEFINITION EXTRAORDINARY—WHAT THE DUTCH THOUGHT OF THE ENGLISH, AND WHAT THE ENGLISH THOUGHT OF THE DUTCH—STORY OF THE CHARTER OAK—WOODEN NUTMEGS INVENTED.

Connecticut is an Indian word and signifies *Long River*. We know, because all the Indian dictionaries we ever read right through give this definition.

In 1636, if our memory serves us, Connecticut was claimed by both the Dutch and English, who had a long dispute about it. Neither faction comprehended what the dispute was about, as the Dutch did not understand English nor the English Dutch. All the Dutch knew was that their antagonists were *tam Yankees*, and the latter were equally clear that theirs were *blarsted Dutchmen* in the worst sense of the word, and thus the matter stood when, fortunately, an interpreter arrived through whom the quarrel was conducted more understandingly. It ended in favor of the English.

The Dutch, it would appear, turned out to be less blarsted than was at first supposed, and, shaking the dust from their wooden shoes, emigrated to New Jersey.

In the year 1636 it occurred to King Charles II to grant Connecticut a charter, which, considered *as* a charter, was a great hit. It gave the people the power to govern themselves. Whenever a Connecticutian traveled abroad folks said, "There goes the Governor of Connecticut," and he really felt himself a man of consequence.

This charter was afterwards annulled by King James II on his accession to the throne, who feared, no doubt, that the people of Connecticut would govern themselves too much, as the population was increasing rapidly. He appointed a Governor from among his poor relations and sent him over to take charge of Connecticut.

Connecticut it seems rather took care of him than otherwise. He varied the monotony of a brief public career by making sundry excursions on rail-back, if we may be allowed the expression, under the auspices of an excited populace. He found the climate too hot to be agreeable, particularly as his subjects presented him with a beautiful Ulster overcoat of cold tar and and goose feathers, and common politeness compelled him to wear it. Need we say the new Governor begged to be recalled?

In the meantime the charter given by Charles II was not destroyed. It was taken care of by Captain Wadsworth, who hid with it in a hollow oak tree, where he remained until the death of the despotic James, which, fortunately, was only about four years, when King William, a real nice man, ascended the throne, and he sat down and wrote to Captain Wadsworth, begging he would not inconvenience himself further on his (William's) account. It was then that the Charter Oak gave back the faded document and Captain Wadsworth, both in a somewhat dilapidated condition.

While confined in the hollow tree the

CHARTER
SECRETING THE CHARTER

Captain beguiled the tedium of restricted liberty by inventing the wooden nutmeg, a number of which he whittled out of bits of wood taken from the walls of his prison. He subsisted almost exclusively upon these during the four years of his voluntary incarceration, and immediately after his release got out a patent on his invention, which he afterwards "swapped" off to a professor in Yale College, who, we understand, made a handsome fortune out of it.

Thus it ever is that patriotism and self-abnegation for the public weal meets with ample reward.

CHAPTER VII.

RHODE ISLAND—ROGER WILLIAMS "DEALT" WITH—A DESPERATE DISSENTER.

Rhode Island was first settled by a desperate character named Roger Williams, who was banished by the Puritans from Massachusetts because he entertained certain inflammatory views decidedly antagonistic to the enjoyment of religious freedom, namely: that all denominations of Christianity ought to be protected in the new colony.

This, of course, was mere heresy upon the face of it, and our forefathers proceeded to "deal" with Brother Williams in the true

OUR
CREED.
THE APOSTACY OF
ROGER WILLIAMS

Puritanic style, when the misguided man bade them a hasty farewell and left on the first train for Rhode Island.

He brought up in a camp of Narragansett Indians, whom he found more liberal in their religious views.

The blind and bigoted Williams, with a few other renegades from the Puritan stronghold, established a colony at the head of Narragansett Bay, which they called Providence.

Other settlements soon sprang up, and the hardened sinner Williams went to England and obtained a charter which united all the settlements into one colony.

At the beginning of the Revolution Rhode Island had a population of 50,000 blinded bigots.

CHAPTER VIII.

NEW HAMPSHIRE—SLIM PICKING—AN EFFECTIVE INDIAN POLICY—JOHN SMITH AGAIN COMES OUT STRONG.

New Hampshire was a sickly child from the first, and of somewhat uncertain parentage. It was claimed by many proprietors, who were continually involved in lawsuits. Its soil was not very fertile, and yielded little else than Indians and lawyers. The former were the most virulent of which any of the colonies could boast, and the latter were of the young and "rising" sort.

These two elements managed to make it extremely lively for the average colonist, who was scalped upon the one hand and

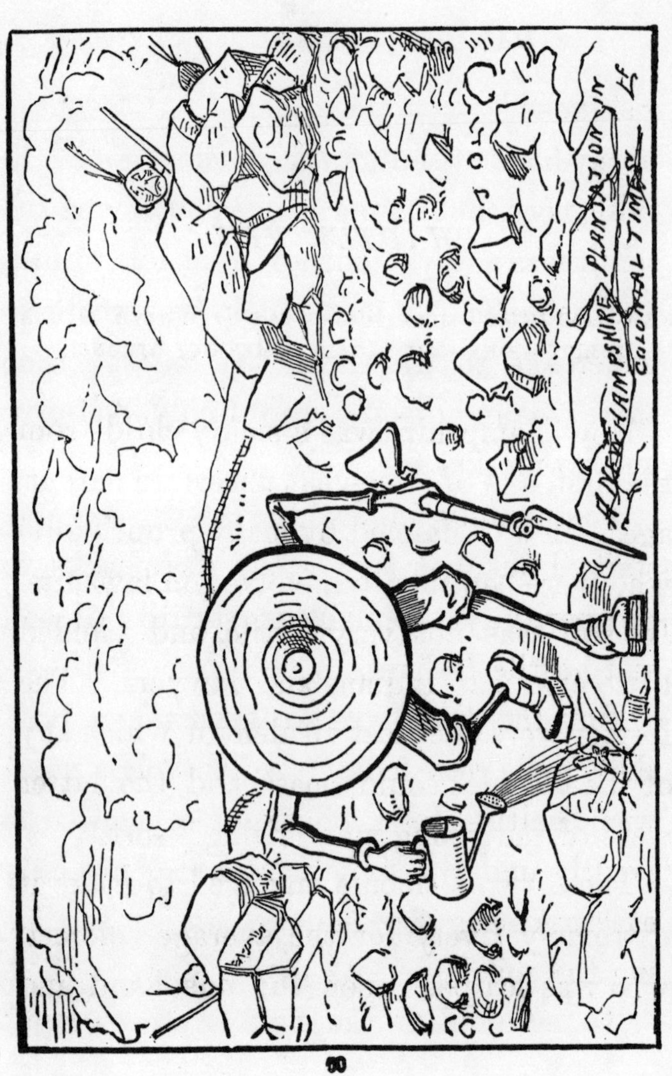
A NEW HAMPSHIRE PLANTATION IN
COLONIAL TIMES
LF

"skinned" upon the other. At first the horny-handed son of toil fondly hoped to raise corn, but owing to the poverty of the soil it was a day's journey from hill to hill, and as much as a man's scalp was worth to undertake to travel it. At harvest time there was an immense crop of cobble stones, and no market for them.

Fortunately, in time the lawyers became starved out, but two great drawbacks to prosperity yet remained; sterility of soil and hostile Indians.

But the time was at hand when both these evils were to be remedied. His name was Smith—John Smith, of course—who readily undertook the contract of not only exterminating the Indians, but of fertilizing the soil.

To accomplish the first of these great

ends, he disguised himself as a medicine man, and went boldly among the noble red men, inducting them into the mysteries of the manufacture and consumption of New England rum. He found them apt pupils, and it was not long before every Red of them, from the biggest sachem to the latest papoose, could not only distill his own fire-water, but drink it, too.

There was soon a very noticeable thinning out in the ranks of the noble red men, and a good deal was said about the setting sun.

The fire-water did its work thoroughly, and the colonists were at length masters of the situation so far as Indians were concerned.

The next thing was to make the land productive. This was a more laborious and tedious undertaking than the first, but

John Smith was equal to the emergency. He caused dirt to be carted from a neighboring State until the rocky surface of New Hampshire was completely covered with a rich sandy loam a foot or two deep. The people raised "some pumpkins" after that, we are informed.

Thus was agriculture established on a solid basis, and New Hampshire made rapid progress.

All honor to John Smith.

CHAPTER IX.

SOME UNRELIABLE STATEMENTS CONCERNING THE EARLY HISTORY OF NEW YORK—TRACES OF A GREAT UNDERTAKING—ADVANCE IN REAL ESTATE—"LOOK HERE UPON THIS PICTURE, AND ON THIS."

New York was discovered in 1609 by one Henry Hudson, an Eglishman by birth, but to all intents and purposes a Dutchman, being then in the service of Holland.

Immediately on his arrival he began the work of building a bridge across the East river, which, it is feared, he never was able to finish. Traces of this quaint structure are plainly to be seen to this day, and have been known, time out of mind, as the "New East River Bridge."

Manhattan Island, upon which New York now stands, was settled by the Dutch, who called it New Netherlands (afterwards New Amsterdam). They bought it of the Indians, paying for the entire island the fabulous sum of twenty-five dollars, and liquidated the purchase with fire-water; but that was before the panic, when there was more "confidence" in business circles than now, and there had been as yet no inflation talk.

New York has changed hands since then, and we understand the property has enhanced in value somewhat. We doubt very much if the island could be bought to-day for double the price originally paid for it, even the way times are now.

Any one comparing the two pictures accompanying this chapter will see how

NEW YORK IN 1620

NEW YORK IN 1876

marvelously we have improved since the days of the Dutch. No. 1 is copied from an old print, dating back to 1620, and is warranted wholly reliable. It is undoubtedly the Sabbath day, for in the foreground is seen an influential citizen of the period, who has come down to the Battery to meditate and fish for eels. He is thinking "How many ages hence will this, his lofty scene, be acted over." Presently he will catch an eel.

Sketch No. 2 is of more recent origin, and was taken from our artist's window. When this picture was first drawn the Brooklyn pier of the bridge was plainly discernible in the background. But since then our landlord, who is a German, and conducts a restaurant on Teutonic principles on the ground floor, has humanely run up a vent-pipe from his kitchen opposite our window, which necessarily excludes the picturesque ruin of the bridge from view. The reader will observe that nothing is now visible but a tall square sheet iron tube and an overpowering sense of garlic, which destroy at once our view and our appetite.

CHAPTER X.

A FLOOD OF HISTORICAL LIGHT IS LET IN UPON NEW JERSEY—ABORIGINES—THE FIRST BOARDING HOUSE—ORGAN-GRINDING AS A FINE ART.

Not many generations ago New Jersey was a buzzing wilderness—howling would be a misnomer, as the tuneful mosquito had it all to himself.

"His right there was none to dispute."

The tuneful mosquito was, in fact, your true New Jersey aboriginal, and we do not hesitate to assert that the wilderness buzzed. But the time came at last when the wilderness of New Jersey was to have something else to do.

In the year (confound it! what year

was it now?) a select company of colonists landed at Hoboken, led by one Philip Carteret. The latter carried with him a large supply of agricultural implements to remind the colonists that they must rely mainly upon the cultivation of cabbages, and devote their energies more or less to the manufacture of Apple Jack for their livelihood. But he soon saw his error, and immediately cabled over for a supply of mosquito nets to instill into their minds the axiom that "self-preservation is the first law of nature."

Mr. Carteret opened a boarding house in Hoboken, to be conducted on strictly temperance principles, and devoted his leisure to the civilizing of the aborigines; but his efforts in this direction were crowned with but partial success.

It is an historical, but not the less melan choly fact, that the aboriginal inhabitants of any country become effete as civilization advances. And thus it happens that, although the mosquito has been handed down to us in modern times, we only behold him in a modified form. That he has not yet entirely lost his sting, the compiler of this work personally ascertained during a four years' exile in Hoboken. For all that the Jersey mosquito of to-day is but an echo, as it were, of his ancestor of colonial times. How thankful should we be then that we were not early settlers.

Hoboken is the capital of New Jersey, and is principally inhabited by Italian barons in disguise, who consecrate their lives exclusively to the study of that king of musical instruments, the barrel-organ.

The Elysian Fields, just north of Hoboken, is a sylvan retreat where the elite of the adjacent cities congregate on Sunday afternoons to play base-ball and strew peanut shells o'er the graves of departed car-horses.

CHAPTER XI.

PENNSYLVANIA SEEN THROUGH A GLASS DARKLY—WM. PENN STANDS TREAT—A STRIKING RESEMBLANCE—HOW TO PRESERVE THE HAIR.

The first colony of Pennsylvania was founded in 1682 by Wm. Penn, a Quaker gentleman of steady habits, who, with remarkable foresight settled at Philadelphia, because he thought it an eligible place to to hold a Centennial Exhibition. He took out naturalization papers, and began by studying the prejudices of the natives with a view to getting upon the good side of them. He smoked the calumet of peace with them and treated them to hard

PENN'S TREATY WITH THE INDIANS
APPLEJACK

cider, under the mellowing influence of which they said he was like "Onas." How well he deserved this compliment the reader will comprehend at once by reference to the accompanying illustration. The coincidence of resemblance is indeed striking, though it must be admitted he is not unlike a cigar sign either.

Wm. Penn bought property in Philadelphia, where he resided for thirty-six years, getting along very well with the neighbors. In proof of which we may mention that in 1718 he went back to England very well off indeed, where he died and was buried in his own hair.

CHAPTER XII.

MARYLAND SETTLED—WHAT'S IN A NAME?—PECULIAR MONETARY SYSTEM.

Lord Baltimore was the oldest inhabitant of Maryland. He named it after Mrs. Charles II, whose maiden name was Henrietta Maria.

The name *Henrietta Marialand* was found rather unhandy for so small a province, so he afterwards cut it down to *Maryland.*

The first settlement was made at the mouth of the Potomac river by a colony of English ladies and gentlemen. They lived chiefly upon green corn and tobacco, which they cultivated in large quantities. When they ran out of funds the latter staple became their currency—the leaf tobacco being the paper money or "greenbacks," and the same dried, mixed with molasses and pressed into blocks or "plugs," represented specie or "hard money." During the growth of the crop it was customary for the capitalist to dig up his stalks every night before going to bed, (previously watering them,) and lock them up in a patent burglar-proof safe, getting up before sunrise next morning to replant them.

The inflation or depression of the money market depended more or less upon the success of the tobacco crop, and as the soil was new there was seldom a panic. One phase of the old Maryland monetary system is graphically set forth on page 79.

"LIQUIDATION"

CHAPTER XIII.

TWO BIRDS KILLED WITH ONE STONE—A COLORED CITIZEN DECLARES HIS INTENTIONS—IN SETTLING NORTH AND SOUTH CAROLINA THE AUTHOR IS HIMSELF UNSETTLED.

The early history of the Carolinas has few cheerful phases. The first settlers were Puritans, who, finding the business unprofitable, sold out and went to speculating in real estate. Preyed upon by speculators and Indians, as Carolina was, few inducements were held out to emigrants of good moral character. Happily, however, about the beginning of the eighteenth century a distinguished colored gentleman poet

A suppositious Early Settler of South Carolina.

ically but forcibly announced his intention of emigrating to North Carolina "Wid de banjo on his knee,"—or was it Alabama? perhaps it was, but no matter. We are positive as to the banjo at any rate. It is a matter of regret that he selected so unagricultural an instrument to begin life with in a new colony.

On page 81 we give a reliable portrait of this individual of color.

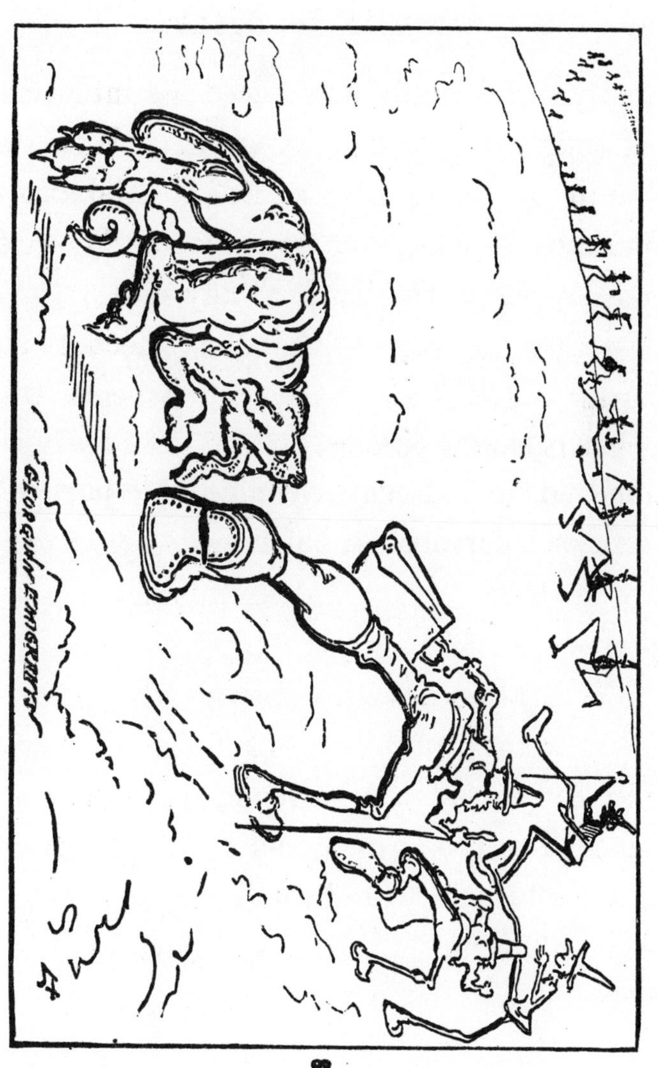
GEORGIAN EMIGRANTS

CHAPTER XIV.

GEORGIA—SLAVERY—A DARK SUBJECT.

Georgia was first settled in 1732 by one hundred and twenty emigrants (not to mention a surreptitious yellow dog that followed them over) led by James Oglethorpe.

Civilization advanced but slowly at first owing to the prohibition of rum and slavery. Twenty years later, however, Georgia was annexed to the Crown, and these two civilizing influences were brought to bear upon society. Georgia made rapid strides after that.

CHAPTER XV.

ENGLISH VS. FRENCH—PURSUIT OF BULL-FROGS UNDER DIFFICULTIES—TRUTH STRANGER THAN FICTION.

Although the English were the oldest inhabitants, it would seem they were not to hold their new possessions undisputed.

The fame of the fledgeling continent spread abroad, and people all over the world packed up their loins and girdled their traveling bags for a journey hither. Even France was suddenly seized with the emigrating fever, and soon became England's principal rival in the new country.

She had heard of the American bull-frog as being the largest in the world, and ere long the banks of the Mississippi from its source to the Gulf were studded with huts whose owners had left their homes in sunny France in quest of frogs and freedom in a foreign clime.

Perched on yonder oscillating snag in mid stream, or wading waist deep in the dismal bayou, armed with fishing tackle, his bronzed forehead furrowed with care and his hook baited with red flannel, the sanguine Gaul sought to tempt the sonorous bull-frog from his native lair. Too often, alas! he surprised the aggressive alligator in *his* native lair, fatally mistaking him for a first-class bull-frog of some rare species. Many an unwary Frenchman was taken in thus, but frogs were hunted with unabated vigor, and every day brought ship-loads of enthusiastic adventurers from the sunny land of France.

So long as the Frenchmen confined themselves to the frogs, (and the alligators confined themselves to the Frenchmen,) their English brethren tolerated them; but when it came to starting opposition corner groceries, and organizing competitive horse-railway companies, (which the French occasionally stepped aside from their legitimate pursuits to do,) they became a positive nuisance, you know. Besides the alligators did not always discriminate between English and French diet. If anything, the epicures of the species seemed to give preference to the former when any train of fortuitous circumstances threw an occasional Englishman in their way.

The duty of the English seemed plainly indicated to them, and they, being in the majority, were not slow in acting up to it,

ENGLISH Vs FRENCH.

by bringing to bear upon their rivals what may be termed an alligator policy. But we leave the rest to our artist, who with a few dashes of his pencil on page 88 has saved us reams of manuscript and barrels of ink. He merely wishes us to explain that the parties on the wharf in the last picture are English, with one exception.

CHAPTER XVI.

THE NAVIGATION ACTS—ILLICIT TOOTHPICKS—A CARGO OF TEA UNLOADED—PORK AND BEANS AS A BEVERAGE—RUMORS OF WARS.

Having seen civilization comfortably settled in its new home, let us see how it conducted itself.

In the year 1660 certain bills were lobbied through the English Parliament which were highly obnoxious to the American colonies then established in Virginia. These were called the Navigation Acts, and prohibited the colonists from sending their pigs to any other market than England, nor allowed them to purchase any article of commerce, not even a toothpick, from any other country, and even that commodity must be ordered from the King himself and delivered in English vessels. If any ingenious colonist was caught whittling a pine splinter or a lucifer match to a point he was looked upon as an outlaw and taken home to England in irons to answer the charge of manufacturing illegal toothpicks. The Navigation Acts were swallowed by the colonists with wry faces for a century or so, and they were beginning to get used to it. But when one fine day the Mother Country invented a new dish, called the "Stamp Act," and began to ladle it out the docile colonists entered their gentle protest.

The Stamp Act provided that the pigs and toothpicks must all bear the government stamp—the stamps, of course, to be paid for by the colonists.

The latter held town meetings, and the district schoolmaster made inflammatory speeches denouncing the British Parliament; the provincial editor hurled defiance in the face of the Crown in a double-leaded article, which he marked with a blue lead pencil and sent to the royal address with his own handwriting. The Crown turned pale, and immediately ordered the Stamp Act to be repealed. It was hoped that this concession would put an end to all hard feelings that had for a long time existed between Parliament and the Town Council of Boston. But now the cry was raised of "No Taxation without Representation," and when one day the news reached Boston that there had been a duty imposed on tea, people took a sudden dislike for that beverage. They said the stamps spoiled the flavor for them, and refused to use it.

As a substitute they consoled themselves with a peculiar infusion called porkinbeans, a well-known Boston beverage.

One day a ship-load of "Best English Breakfast" arrived at the wharf, and all Boston picturesquely arrayed in Indian costume turned out to unload it. In the excitement of the moment the caddies were accidentaly tossed over the wrong side of the ship, the stamps having previously been canceled by the absent-minded citizens.

Great Britain immediately sent over several ship-loads of troops, but these were scarcely less obnoxious than the cargo of stamped tea, especially as they asked some

TEA OVERBOARD

very embarassing questions relative to the careless unloading of said cargo.

Patrick Henry, a member of the Virginia Legislature, took it upon himself to return a rather evasive answer by "repeating it, sir, WE MUST FIGHT!"

CHAPTER XVII.

REVOLUTIONARY—A ROW AT CONCORD—A MASTERLY RETREAT—THE BRITISH COUNT NOSES.

And we did fight.

The first gun was fired on the 19th of April, 1775, at Concord, where a large and select assortment of explosives for celebrating the coming Fourth of July was stored and guarded by a squad of minute-men.

A detachment of 3,000 British was sent to destroy these explosives.

"Disperse ye Rebels!" is what the British commander remarked.

"You're another!" promptly replied the minute-men, and immediately obeyed the

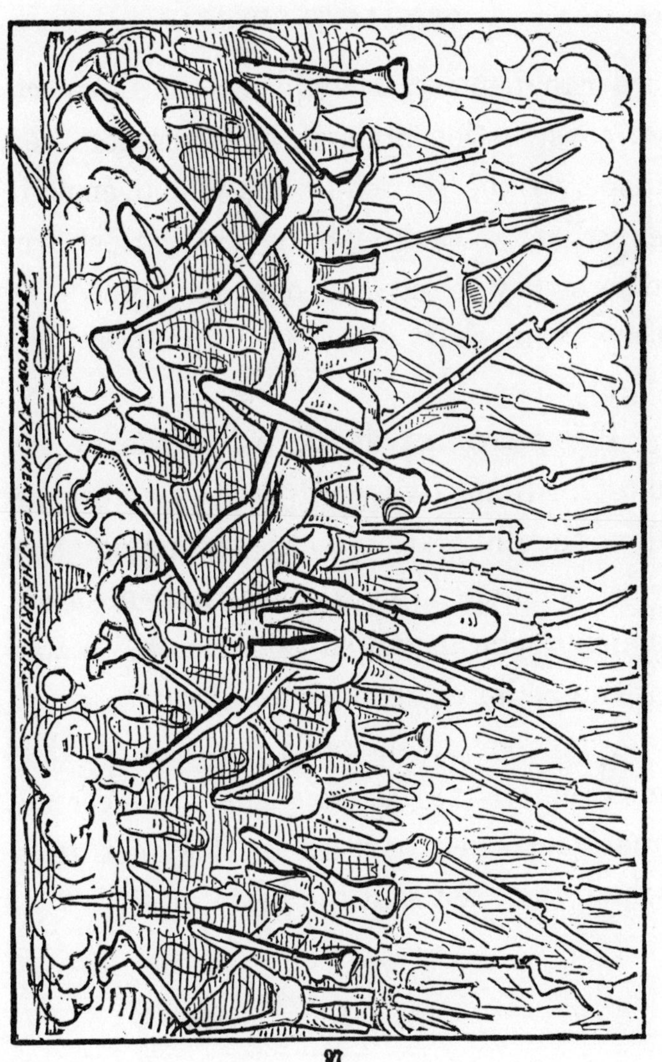
LEXINGTON — A RETREAT OF THE BRITISH

order to disperse. They placed an unexpected construction upon it, however, for they dispersed the British troops, who deemed it expedient to saunter back to Charlestown, where they found on counting noses that they were short some two hundred and eighty men.

This retreat of the British is one of the most brilliant on record, and, if we can believe the illustration on the preceding page, was conducted in a somewhat informal manner. The unstudied yet animated action of the pedal extremities speaks of a pressing engagement suddenly remembered that must not be neglected. There are certain anatomical peculiarities in this picture of which the least said the better.

CHAPTER XVIII.

FULL ACCOUNT OF THE BATTLE OF BUNKER HILL—FALSE TEETH AND HEROISM—ARE REPUBLICS UNGRATEFUL?

About two months after the events narrated in the last chapter the battle of Bunker Hill took place, June 19, 1775. It was conducted by General Bunker upon the American side, while one General Hill led the British.

On this memorable occasion the Americans managed to destroy a thousand or so of the enemy, and might have done better had their supply of bullets held out. These becoming exhausted the noble fellows fell back upon the brass buttons of their uniforms, which they fired at the British as long as there was a button left among them.

The brave Bunker, when his stock of buttons gave out, bethought him of his false teeth. He removed them from his mouth, and with fire in his eye and a horse-pistol in his right hand, (holding on his buttonless uniform with his left,) he turned upon the enemy a galling fire of "store" teeth, and every one of them took effect, making sixteen of the red-coats bite the dust.

In his official report of the battle which he sent to Congress the heroic man avers: that, if there had been a dentist handy to extract 'em, he would have sacrificed every dashed natural tooth in his head for the cause of Liberty.

BAKED BEANS
PORTRAIT OF MR BUNKER
PORTRAIT OF MR HILL
BUNKER-HILL MONUMENT

As a reward for his heroic conduct, Congress had him measured for a new set of elegant silver-mounted molars, which it promised to present to him some day with an appropriate inscription. And yet they say Republics are ungrateful!

For further information regarding this great battle, see illustration. There was a monument erected upon the spot to commemorate the battle, and should you ever go to Boston you will probably be asked, "Have you tried our baked beans, and have you seen Bunker Hill monument?"

CHAPTER XIX.

STILL REVOLUTIONARY–THE FIRST FOURTH OF JULY TAKES PLACE—DECLARATION OF INDEPENDENCE—AN ABLE DOCUMENT—PARLIAMENT IS MUCH MOVED AND GETS OUT YELLOW HANDBILLS.

One hot sultry day in the summer of 1776 Thomas Jefferson eased his mind in an essay called the Declaration of Independence, which said in effect that the United Colonies of America had saved up money enough to start in business for themselves, and henceforth there was to be no connection with over the way. This document, dated July 4, 1776, was signed by John Hancock and a few other members

DECLARATION OF INDEPENDENCE.

John Hancock

Edward Rutledge

George Wythe
Richard Henry Lee
Th Jefferson
Benj. Harrison
Thos Nelson jr.
Francis Lightfoot Lee
Carter Braxton
Josiah Bartlett
Wm Whipple
Saml Adams
John Adams
Robt Treat Paine
Elbridge Gerry
Step. Hopkins
William Ellery
Roger Sherman
Saml Huntington
Wm Williams
Oliver Wolcott
Matthew Thornton

Abra Clark
Robt Morris
Benjamin Rush
Benj. Franklin
John Morton
Geo Clymer
Jas Smith
Geo. Taylor
James Wilson
Geo. Ross
Caesar Rodney
Geo Read
Tho M:Kean

Phil. Livingston
Saml Lewis
Lewis Morris
Geo Walton
Button Gwinnett
Wm Hooper
Joseph Hewes
John Penn

of Congress who had learned to write, and was duly published in all the daily papers. We received a marked copy of one of the papers in which it appeared at the time, and with a sort of vague instinct that we might find it useful some day, cut it out and preserved it with religious care. We reproduce it here in fac-simile.

It will be found to be a very readable article, and we advise our readers to peruse it carefully, if they have to skip all the rest of the book. The gentlemen who signed the Declaration have courteously furnished us their autographs, which we also take the liberty of placing before our readers.

When the attention of Parliament was accidentally called to this article, in one of the papers above alluded to, its feelings may be more readily imagined than described. And when that quaint old fossil Disraeli put on his spectacles and read it "out loud" there was not a dry eye in the house. Parliament cried like a child, or, more properly, like a whole orphan asylum. Becoming calmer after awhile they got out immense illustrated yellow posters, representing an enraged lion engaged in bitter discussion with a sanguinary one-eared mule, and after stating that this was the Lion and the Unicorn, the poster went on to say that the Americans were rebels and humbugs, and further cautioned the public against selling them goods on credit.

When these handbills were posted conspicuously and profusely on every stone wall, barn, and rail-fence in America, the spirit of '76 rose to several per cent. above proof. War was declared, and General

Washington was appointed commander-in-chief of the Continental army.

He gave strict orders to place none but Americans on guard, while England sent more troops to America, and expected every man to do his duty.

CHAPTER XX.

REVOLUTIONARY AS BEFORE—"PLACE NONE BUT AMERICANS ON GUARD TO NIGHT"—CHRISTMAS FESTIVITIES—ALMOST A VICTORY—A BRITISHER SHOWS WASHINGTON GREAT DISRESPECT—WASHINGTON CROSSING THE DELAWARE.

One dark, cold winter's night General Washington issued very strict orders indeed relative to guard mounting, and each sentinel had to either show his naturalization papers or give affidavit of American parentage.

The British hordes were encamped just across the Delaware river in numbers greatly superior to the Americans, and were only waiting for the river to freeze over in order that they might skate across and capture the entire Continental army. As there was no immediate prospect of that, however, owing to the mildness of the weather, and having much spare time on their hands, the Britons improved their minds by the study of High-low-Jack and other branches of science.

It was Christmas night, and the whole army had been celebrating the day in good old English style. Every minion of them had inhaled more or less commissary whisky, and as night approached had succumbed to its sedative qualities.

General Washington saw how it would be, and announced his intention of spending the evening out, without entering into further particulars. He borrowed a log canoe of one of the neighbors and paddled across the river amid floating ice and made the whole army prisoners. The difficulty now arose of getting the booty home. The British army by actual count turned out to be much larger than Washington had anticipated, and he began to entertain serious doubts as to whether the small canoe would accommodate so many.

While he stood thus enjoying his triumph, and deliberating as to what course to pursue next, an able-bodied Britisher manifested unmistakable symptoms of returning animation by raising himself on one elbow, and demanding in a loud voice of the Father of his Country what the highly colored blazes the blarsted old three-cornered pig-tail meant by loafing about there, and then ordered him in an incoherent manner to "roll in another bar'l, and be quick about it."

With that coolness of deliberation which characterized all his public acts, Washington hastily withdrew, leaving his prisoners to be called for at some future time.

A few days later, taking advantage of a sudden cold snap, he crossed the Delaware once more, taking a small army with him to assist in bringing his prisoners home. The latter had so far recovered from the effects of Christmas as to make a stout resistance, and the battle of Trenton took place, resulting in favor of the Americans.

Washington crossing the Delaware furnished a very good subject for a very bad painting, which may be seen among other bad paintings in the Rotunda of the Capitol at Washington. At first sight this work of art might be mistaken for an advertising dodge of some enterprising ice company,

WASHINGTON CROSSING
THE DELAWARE

but there is not the slightest doubt it is meant to bear an historical, not a commercial significance.

On page 112 will be found a reliable version of the incident briefly sketched, which our artist is willing to work up in oil for the Government if Congress will make a suitable appropriation and agree to furnish a barrel of oil and a few acres of canvas.

Sealed proposals addressed to care of the publishers of this work will be promptly considered.

CHAPTER XXI.

MORE REVOLUTIONARY THAN EVER—LIVELY TIMES AT A WATERING-PLACE—THE STARS AND STRIPES INVENTED.

On the 17th of October, 1777, General Washington surrounded and captured the British army under Burgoyne at Saratoga, where they had been spending the Summer, and where it strikes us they had remained rather late in the season.

The British were entirely out of provisions, and had been living exclusively on congress water for some weeks past. Mr. Burgoyne had written home to the Crown that, if the war was to be successfully

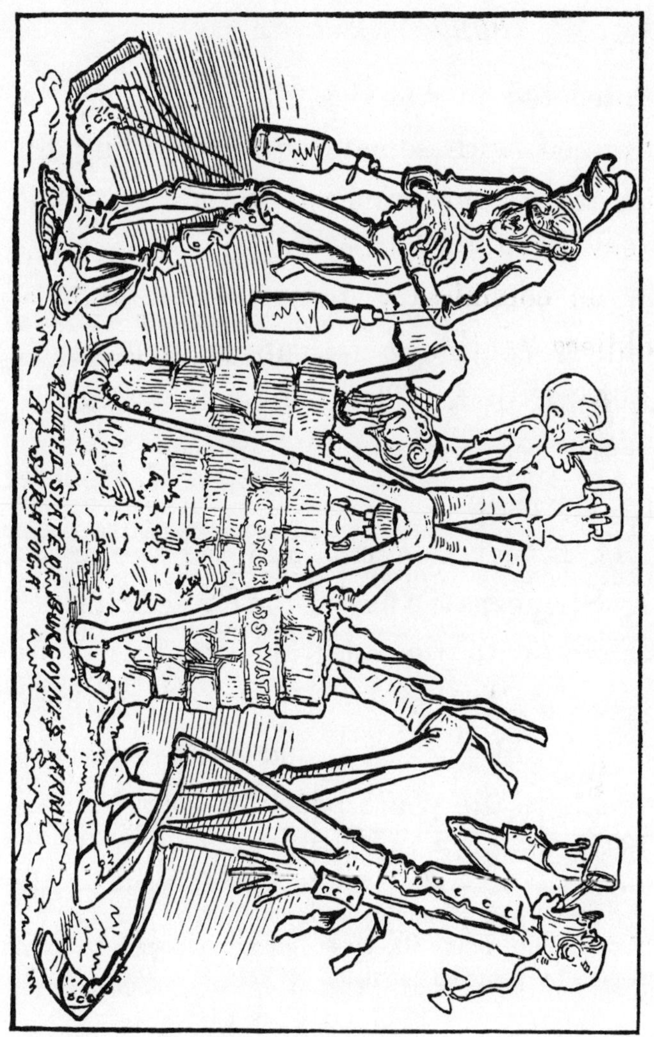

REDUCED STATE OF BURGOYNE'S ARMY AT SARATOGA.

prosecuted in America, the army must be supplied with something more filling for the price than mineral water. But he must have forgotten to mail the letter, for no commissary stores arrived, and the soldiers continued to subsist upon their aqueous diet. They were consequently greatly reduced and fell an easy prey to the Americans.

That year Congress adopted the Stars and Stripes as the flag of the United States,* which (with the addition of other stars from time to time) has been handed down to grateful posterity, and to-day proudly reveals to the youth of a free Republic the whereabouts of the circus tent.

---

* NOTE.—This supplied a want long felt, as the army had hitherto rallied round Mr. Washington's red pocket handkerchief tied to a broom handle.

CHAPTER XXII.

IMPRUDENT CONDUCT OF BENEDICT ARNOLD—A REAL ESTATE SPECULATION—$50,000 THE PRICE OF LIBERTY (TERMS CASH)—MAJOR ANDRÉ IS SERIOUSLY COMPROMISED—SUSPENSE—EVIL COMMUNICATION—A TALE-BEARING YELLOW DOG.

It was in the fall of 1780 that one Benedict Arnold, being seriously inconvenienced for want of funds, employed some very questionable means of getting on his financial legs again. After laying his head together for a spell, he resolved to realize on some real estate belonging to the colonial government, and make a European tour on the proceeds.

He secretly negotiated with the British

Commander, Lord Clinton, (then at New York,) for the sale of a few acres at West Point, where he (Arnold) happened to be in command, which he agreed to transfer to the said Lord Clinton for and in consideration of $50,000 to him, the said Arnold, paid in hand.

It is true, the property was occupied by Government as a military post of some importance, and was the repository of valuable stores and munitions of war, and besides the nucleus of the American army was garrisoned there. But Arnold was too much of a man of business to let a little drawback of that sort stand between him and a bargain. He said he would throw all these in if the other party was willing. The other party good-naturedly agreed to overlook all draw-

BENEDICT ARNOLD MEDITATING
TREASON
MR ARNOLD ABANDONS
HIS PLANS
CAPTURE OF MAJOR ANDRÉ
MAJOR ANDRÉ ABANDONS HIS PLANS.
MR ANDRÉ IN
A STATE OF SUSPENSE.

backs, and sent his man Friday, Major André, to close the bargain and bring the property home. After a very pleasant interview with Arnold behind a haystack, which resulted to the satisfaction of both, Major André started for New York with the title-deed for the newly acquired property safely stowed away in his left coat-tail pocket. He had proceeded some distance on his journey when he was stopped by three American gentlemen whom he met, and who, with that unhappy inquisitiveness to which their race is notoriously predisposed, desired information as to whence he had come, whither he was going, and what "line" he was in.

The Major, with great ingenuity, replied that he was a representative of the press from New York, and had been to headquarters to interview General Washington as to what he thought his chances were in the coming presidential canvass, and whether he, as an honest man, really considered himself a fit person to be entrusted with an army? and if it were true, as had been represented, that he advocated the introduction of the new breech-loading umbrellas into the army as a military measure? whether he was not afraid of hurting himself with his sword, or putting somebody's eyes out by the careless habit he had of pointing out beauties in the landscape (see equestrian portraits) with that weapon? also whether he had any chewing tobacco?

However plausibly the Major's account of himself might strike most people, it failed to satisfy those to whom it was addressed.

They said they had at first merely looked upon him as a suspicious character, but now, by his own confessed connection with the press, they could not regard him in any other light than that of a very dangerous person, to say the least, and they must trouble him to turn his pockets inside out.

With tears in his eyes he took from his pockets an oroide watch, a jackknife, and some Erie railway shares.

"Let me go hence," he said, in a voice choked with emotion, "and these shall be your guerdons; there is just a guerdon apiece. You can toss up among you for the choice."

But, although his captors happened to be wealthy capitalists, they declined to add to their means at the expense of honor.

They said guerdons were out of their line, and demanded to know if he (the Major) could discern anything of a verdant tinge in their optics. The Major could not for the life of him. One of these low fellows then hinted that he more than suspected the true nature of their (now) prisoner, and he must be investigated, and further, by a very expressive pantomime (catching himself by the throat, opening his eyes very wide, protruding his tongue and breathing hard) tried to convey some idea of what would happen if his suspicions should prove correct.

The gallant Major was never so mortified in his life before. He began to wonder what would ever become of him if these vulgar persons into whose hands he had fallen should really so far misconstrue his conduct as to condemn him for a spy?

* * * * * * * * * * *

He was not kept long in suspense. (See illustration on page 119.)

There is one incident in connection with *André's* capture which has always been unaccountably overlooked by other historians, and which if we omitted in this place we should feel that we had not conscientiously discharged our duty.

When Major André found himself a captive he felt that it would be very desirable to communicate with Arnold before their transactions should be made public. He also saw the impossibility of reaching him by telegraph, as that means of correspondence was not to be invented until half a century or more later, and to delay so long as that might be fatal. While casting about for some means of giving warning to his friend, his eye chanced to rest upon a specimen of the canine species of the yellow persuasion belonging to one of his captors, and a ray of hope gleamed in upon his soul.

They had halted for the night, intending to proceed with the prisoner to headquarters next morning, and preparations were being made for supper. An empty tin coffee-pot sat near the fire, and the yellow dog sat near the tin coffee-pot blinking at the fire, his mind evidently absorbed in some abstruse canine problem. By a curious, though perhaps natural association of ideas, the Briton saw here the crude materials for communicating with Arnold ready to his hand.

Pretending to make an entry in his diary he hastily scribled off these lines:

"Friend Benedict:

Owing to circumstances over which I have no control, I am unable to take any further steps in that little matter of ours at present; the boys have in point of fact scooped me. You would have been a better man in my place. Hoping to meet you in the happy hunting grounds, I am yours, in limbo,

ANDRÉ.

P.S.—By the way, hadn't you better drop in upon our mutual friend General Clinton at New York and remain with him for a few days until it blows over? I only throw this out as a mere suggestion. Good bye. A."

Watching his opportunity when his captors' backs were turned, the Major slipped this epistle into the coffee-pot, clapped on the lid, and, having diverted the canine's attention by means of a piece of salt pork, which had been originally laid out for the approaching meal, hastily appended the tin vessel to his caudal extremity, and having with nice precision turned the animal's nose in the direction of Arnold's tent, he gave the tail an agonizing twist, and—and the party did without coffee that night.

The yellow dog came duly to hand, and Mr. Arnold was not slow in acting upon the hint contained in the message he brought. With that long-headedness which is the characteristic of the true man of business he anticipated any investigation of his conduct that might follow by resigning and changing his residence at once. We learn that he subsequently went to

INSTANCE OF CANINE SAGACITY.

Europe, but up to the present writing has not yet returned.

If any one doubts the incident we have just related about the way in which the news of André's capture reached Arnold, he has only to narrowly scrutinize our illustration, which treats of the moment when the sagacious quadruped reaches the American lines. With almost human intelligence he overturns the sentinel, who, doubtful of the nature of his business, has challenged his further progress.

For Mr. Arnold's own sake we regret the imprudent course he pursued to improve the state of his exchequer. It is true his funds were low, and no one can blame him for wanting to make a "raise." But then he ought to have remembered that there are always honest as well as lucrative pur suits open to the deserving poor involving but small investments; for instance, he might have started a paper, peddled matches, got an appointment in the Cabinet, blacked boots, organized savings banks, or written comic histories.

We are aware that these invaluable suggestions come too late to apply specifically to Mr. Arnold's case, but we do hope that all who have invested capital in this book will shape their course by the few hints we have here thrown out, and above all remember that the plucking out of even the tail feathers of the American Eagle for commercial purposes is ever attended with risk. * * * * *

On a more thorough investigation of the subject we learn that Benedict Arnold is dead, and has been for some time; but he lives in American history.

CHAPTER XXIII.

THE AFFAIRS OF THE REVOLUTION WOUND UP—CORNWALLIS STEPS DOWN AND OUT.

Cornwallis, commander of the British forces, placed his sword at the disposal of General Washington on the 19th of October, 1781, and took passage on the next steamer for Europe.

The final scene in the history of the war for American liberty is graphically set forth on page 132. It is copied from a group of wax-works illustrative of that event, and is, therefore, warranted reliable.

The war was now virtually over, but it was not until two years later that England

"SURRENDER OF CORNWALLIS"

signed a quit-claim deed resigning all right and title to its American property.

The Continental army was disbanded, and returning to their homes the soldiers hammered their muskets and things into plowshares and sold them to the farmers. The battle fields were cut up into corner lots, and a season of great prosperity began. Washington was elected President of the young Republic, and gave great satisfaction in that capacity. His second term having expired, he wrote an address of great literary merit and retired to private life at Mount Vernon. He ingeniously forged a little hatchet out of his sword for his little step-son, and taught him how to chop down cherry trees with neatness and dispatch and own up to it afterwards.

G. W. ENJOYING THE REPOSE OF PRIVATE LIFE

CHAPTER XXIV.

AN INCIDENT OF THE REVOLUTION.

It is always very noble and all that sort of thing when a nation or individuals sacrifice anything for a principle. Sometimes such sacrifice meets with immediate reward and sometimes the reward is delayed and the parties making the sacrifice have to wait indefinitely for their pay. A little incident which befel an ancestor of ours illustrates both these propositions to some extent, and having a few moments to spare we are tempted to relate it briefly, as follows.

On one memorable occasion, in pursuance of Washington's famous order to place none but Americans on guard, an ancestor of ours was detailed to guard certain military stores. The missiles of destruction, it will be noticed, were flying about in a style that seemed more promiscuous than soothing to a nervous temperament.

Accidents will happen in the best regulated families, and it certainly was no fault of our ancestor that a shell, fired by unprincipled Britons, struck the military stores aforesaid, destroying them, but, beyond giving a severe shock to his nervous system, the projectile did our ancestor no harm as it did not explode.

As a reward for his valiant conduct, Washington begged our ancestor to accept the unexploded shell, which the latter resolved to preserve as a souvenir of the adventure and hand down to posterity.

He carried it with him on many a weary march.

'Tis true he found it a serious inconvenience ofttimes.

But he remembered posterity and pressed on

Here we see him handing the relic down to posterity.

In after years posterity handed it over to an obnoxious female relative, who irreverently used it as a candlestick.

On one occasion obnoxious female relative imprudently went to sleep, allowing the candle to burn low in its socket.

Need we say that posterity's obnoxious female relative got what she had often given him,—a severe blowing up?

CHAPTER XXV.

THIS HISTORY DABBLES IN POLITICS MUCH AGAINST ITS WISHES—PRELIMINARY OBSERVATIONS—A CHAPTER OF ACCIDENTS AND PRESIDENTS—"LIVES OF GREAT MEN ALL REMIND US."

We have always from childhood's hour instinctively recoiled from politics, and have thus far managed to keep out of Congress. If with equal success we can manage to keep out of jail for the rest of our natural existence we shall feel that life has not altogether been a failure. (This is what is called genuine broad American humor. If the reader can find nothing in it to excite his risibilities after a reasonable trial his money will be refunded.)

When it first reached the ears of the present Administration through the Librarian of Congress, to whom we applied for a copyright, that we were about to publish a history of our native land, we received per return mail a letter signed by the Administration, asking us if we would accept the appointment of U. S. Minister to the South Sea Islands. This office had just been made vacant by the circumstance of the last incumbent having participated in a public banquet given in honor of his arrival at his consulate, and being himself the principal ingredient of a certain savory *ragout*, his presence there, it would seem, proved fatal, and it was his place which we were invited to supply.

We returned a somewhat evasive answer. We never voted but once in our life, and that was at a presidential election soon after reaching our majority. We voted for ——, but no matter. To offend party prejudice at this time might be fatal to our hopes. The day after the election we received a bill of two dollars for "poll-tax," which the collector said we owed and we had better pay or have our body lodged in the county jail until we should call for it, and settle up what was due on it to the State. The unprincipled man had obtained our address from the registry books, and this our first ebulition of patriotism cost us two dollars.

However much inclined we may be by nature and experience to avoid the subject of politics as a rule, it now becomes our duty to make mention of certain exponents of American politics, but whether to their ad vantage or disadvantage will depend entirely upon the record they have left behind them.

We take it for granted, (you may have noticed that a great deal is taken for granted in this book,) that the reader is already acquainted with the duties of the President of the United States. If not, let him lose no time in reading up on the subject, for we are all liable at any moment to be nominated to the office, and it would be dreadfully mortifying not to know how to go to work.

We have seen in the preceeding chapters how liberty was planted on American soil, but the crop must be watched and taken care of, and for this duty the office of PRESIDENT was created. Eighteen different persons have successively undertaken the contract of guarding the crop sown by our forefathers, and in one or two instances, we regret to say, these have turned out to be mere scarecrows, and sorry ones at that.

This scathing remark is not intended to apply to

GEORGE WASHINGTON,

who, as we have already shown, was the first President of the United States, and who did as well as could be expected for a first attempt. In fact, George did well whatever he undertook to do, and we have no complaint to make in these pages against him.

On page 151 will be found some illustrated particulars concerning this great man's life, which our readers, young and old, will do well to imitate. The series of silhouettes at the top of the page treat of the Story of the Little Hatchet.

1
2
3
4
HERE
Feb 22nd 1732
GEO. WASHINTON
WAS BORN
PAINT
USE
BINKS'
BABY-DROPS
CHILDREN
CRY FOR IT
5
6
7

No. 1. Here we see the Grandfather of his Country climbing a cherry tree after cherries.

No. 2. His little son (afterwards Father of his Country) is here seen chopping at said tree with his little hatchet.

No. 3. How should he know that the old man was up said tree, and if so, what business had he up there anyhow?

No. 4. "I'll let you know," is what the old gentleman remarked. "I did it with my little hatchet," roared George as well as he could from his embarrassing position, "but I'll never do so no more!"

Advice gratis. When you chop down cherry trees wait until the old man goes out of town.

No. 5. Gives us a fine view of the site of

Washington's birthplace, and shows what an enterprising man Dr. Binks is.

No. 6. The crop of persons who have nursed and otherwise remember Washington is pretty good this year.

No. 7. Here we have a party who does *not* remember Washington to any great extent. Thinks he has heard the name somewhere.

"O piteous spectacle!"

Washington's immediate successor was

JOHN ADAMS,

who was inaugurated March 4, 1797. He displayed superior capacity for the position by removing the national capital from Philadelphia to Washington, where it has remained ever since. It was a good riddance for Philadelphia, but rather severe on Washington.

PUBLIC DOCUMENTS
MR. ADAMS REMOVING THE
CAPITOL TO WASHINGTON

Mr. Adams only served one term. He was naturally a little *piqued* at not being nominated the second time, and retiring to Quincy, Mass., he started an opposition post office, where he passed his declining years.

Thomas Jefferson

was the third President of the United States. He was a gentleman of fine literary attainments, his most popular works being the Declaration of Independence and a humorous poem called "Beautiful Snow." He wrote the latter during the winter of 1798, (which was the most severe of any within the memory of the oldest inhabitant,) working on it of nights. He served two terms, and in the Spring of 1809 went to work on a farm, where he spent the sun-

Thomas Jefferson
destroying
Potato bugs

set of his days cultivating potatoes. He said it was easier than being President, and a great deal more respectable.

James Madison

next took charge of the helm of State, and very unsettled weather he found it for a new beginner.

During his Administration the country became involved in another war with Great Britain, growing out of certain liberties taken by the latter with American vessels upon the high seas.

Whenever an English man-of-war ran short of hands its commander simply helped himself from the crew of any American merchantman he happened to encounter. James Madison stood it as long as he could, and then declared war. This was called the "War of Twelve," (afterwards increased to several thousand,) and lasted two years.

Commodore Perry met the enemy on the Erie canal on the 10th of September, 1814, and after a spirited naval battle they were his property.

☞ See illustration.

JAMES MONROE

woke up one fine morning in 1817 and found himself President of the United States. He set his wits to work and invented the "Monroe Doctrine," a neat and ingenious contrivance for preventing any foreign Power from starting branch houses in America. He got it patented.

Mr. Monroe declined a third term on account of the cry of "Cæsarism" having been raised by a rural journal. On retiring

PERRY'S VICTORY ON THE
ERIE CANAL.

THE MONROE DOCTRINE.

from public life Mr. Monroe entered upon literary pursuits, and wrote some very able dime novels. His master-piece, called "The Poisoned Peanut, or the Ghostly Goblin of the Gory Glen," has been translated into every language.

JOHN QUINCY ADAMS,

of Massachusetts, next tried on the presidential shoes (1825). Business being dull, Mr. Adams whitewashed the Presidential Mansion, (a barrel of lime having been appropriated by Congress,) since which time it has been known as the White House.

Mr. Adams conducted himself in a gentlemanly manner, kept good hours, and paid his board regularly.

ANDREW JACKSON

was next called to the chair. Mr. Jackson

PRESIDENT ADAMS
MAKES HIMSELF
USEFUL

lived chiefly upon hickory nuts, and it was in recognition of this well-known fact that he was affectionately nicknamed "Old Hickory" by his admirers.

He sometimes made use of very forcible language, and on more than one occasion was distinctly heard to swear, "by the eternal JINGO, the Constitution must and shall be preserved!"

Mr. Jackson had been elected on the Democratic ticket.

In our illustration Mr. Jackson is seen climbing a shell-bark hickory tree in quest of his favorite luxury. The portrait is striking. The shirt collar especially will be recognized by all who held office under this remarkable man.

MARTIN VAN BUREN

was inaugurated March 4, 1837. A finan-

OLD MR. HICKORY.

çial crash, called the panic of '37, immediately followed, so it is to be feared that Martin was a bad financier. If we had been elected in his stead we would have adopted an entirely different financial policy.

The disastrous results of Van Buren's Administration are painfully apparent in the illustration on page 166.

Harrison—Tyler.

William Henry Harrison moved into the White House March 4, 1841. He died just one month after, and Vice-President John Tyler stepped into his shoes. He put his foot in it, however, and astonished the party who had elected him (the Whigs) by his vetoing talents. He rather overdid it in the case of a bill passed by Congress

HARD TIMES
IN '37

to establish United States banks, and every member of his Cabinet resigned excepting Dan. Webster, who was then too busily engaged on his dictionary to think of making out a resignation.

President Tyler was a handsome man but a bad manager.

James K. Polk

was elected on the Democratic ticket, by a large majority, in 1844, and managed to get into a row with Mexico by admitting Texas into the Union soon after his accession to the chair. Mexico set up a frivolous claim to the territory, which, owing to the prompt measures adopted by Mr. Polk, she was unable to establish.

The war which followed between the United States and Mexico was short but

WHY DAN WEBSTER DID NOT RESIGN.

sanguinary, as the reader will admit on reference to our illustration, which, aside from its historical value, gives those of us who have never served our country an excellent opportunity of seeing how a battle is conducted without incurring any unneccessary risk. Whoever can look upon this fearful scene of carnage without having the cold chills run down his back must be stony hearted indeed. We would not like to board in the same block with such a person. Even as we write we fancy we can smell the sulphuric vapors of burning powder, but that after all may be only the German restaurant below getting dinner ready.

With the exception of certain little eccentricities of character, (hardly worth mentioning,) Mr. Polk proved a very

BIRDS-EYE VIEW OF THE MEXICAN WAR.

desirable tenant of the White House, and on retiring left it in good repair.

TAYLOR—FILLMORE.

Zachary Taylor took the White House off Mr. Polk's hands, but only survived six months.

Vice-President Millard Fillmore succeeded him, and having by accident discovered that there was a good deal of gold secreted about California, recognized the importance of admitting her into the Union lest some foreign Power should take it into its head to carry off the rich territory some dark night. There was special danger to be apprehended from China, which had already begun to make excavations from below. President Fillmore lost no time in taking California in, and many ambitious young gentlemen of culture went there and grew

A YOUNG GENTLEMAN OF CULTURE ON HIS WAY TO CALIFORNIA.

up with the country. In the work of art on page 172, we behold one of the latter journeying toward the setting sun, accompanied by as many of the luxuries of civilization as his limited means of transportation will admit of.

There seem to be one or two incongruities in this otherwise master-piece which we are at a loss how to reconcile with known laws of science. We allude more particularly to the phenomenon of the sun and moon shining simultaneously. But for the artist's usual respectful way of treating serious subjects we should be inclined to suspect that he was trifling with our feelings. The worst of it is, the paradox escaped our notice until after the plates had been cast. We hope our artist will be able to explain it away on his return from Rome

JAMES BUCHANAN

next undertook to fill the vacancy. Nature abhors a vacuum, and generally fills it with wind if it can do no better. Republics sometimes imitate her example, and the election of Mr. Buchanan was a case in point. He was chronically afflicted with "squatter sovereignity," and spent most of his time in trying to comprehend American politics.

During Buchanan's Administration John Brown and Sons undertook the contract of exterminating slavery, and as an initial step seized and burned the United States Arsenal at Harper's Ferry. But the firm failed before the job was half completed.

Mr. Brown's body now lies mouldering in the grave, but it is due to him to state that his soul goes marching on.

JOHN BROWNS SOUL
IN THE ACT OF
MARCHING
ON

On a previous page will be found John Brown's soul in the act of marching. Our artist was unable to obtain a very exact sketch as it was getting quite dark.

LINCOLN—JOHNSON.

Abraham Lincoln was next voted into the chair, which reminds us of a little anecdote.

Some years ago an Erie canal boat was weighing anchor in the harbor of New York preparatory to setting sail for Buffalo, when the Captain was hailed by a weary wayfarer, who said he wanted to go to Buffalo, and having no money was willing to work his passage. The heart of the old salt was touched; a tear stole down his weather-beaten cheek, and he allowed the poor man to lead one of the mules on the tow-path all the way to Buffalo.

A "HUNDRED DAYS'" MAN PUTTING DOWN THE REBELLION.

Abraham Lincoln was willing to work his passage. He earned every cent of his salary, and rendered services to humanity which humanity will not soon forget. Soon after his inauguration, in 1861, the Southern rebellion broke out, which was eventually put down by the "hundred days' men." On page 179 will be found some cheerful particulars of the war between the North and South, the more somber details of which we leave to other and abler pens and pencils.

Vice-President Andrew Johnson succeeded Mr. Lincoln. with somewhat doubtful success. As Mr. Johnson was a tailor by education he seemed to be the man of all others cut out for the place; but his subsequent conduct gave rise to conflicting opinions on this subject. He became the unfor

FORT SUMTER FIRED UPON
BATTLE OF BULL RUN
EMANCIPATION
A 3 MONTHS MAN WISHING THIS CRUEL WAR WERE OVER
MARY JONES
CAPTURE OF JEFF DAVIS

tunate proprietor of a "policy"* which gave Congress a good deal of trouble. Near the expiration of his official career he got a leave of absence, and "swung around the circle," (as he himself expressed it,) making speeches in which he compared himself to Andrew Jackson and seriously compromised himself by shamelessly admitting that he had held every office in the gift of the people, from Alderman of his native village to President of the United States.

During Mr. Johnson's Administration he had more woes on account of Congress

"Than wars or women have."

Mr. Johnson would gladly have dispensed

---

* NOTE.—We have tried in vain to procure a ground plan of this "policy," hence we are unable to furnish any illustration to this branch of our subject.

with Congress. Indeed, on one occasion he made an attempt to impeach that body, but failed by one vote.

Ulysses S. Grant

was put under bonds to keep the peace March 4th, 1869. He served two terms, and went abroad to avoid a third.

Rutherford B. Hayes

was induced to move into the White House by the promise of new paint, and repairs to the front gate. Mrs. Hayes has proved a model housekeeper, but she declares she can neither abide nor displace the aroma of Grant's cigar. Justice to Mr. Hayes compels us to report good crops during his administration. He will not be a candi-

THE PRESENT INCUMBENT.

date for reëlection. A rumor is afloat that he and his illustrious predecessor will buy the New York *Sun*, proposing to run it in the interests of conciliation.

As soon as we ascertain who is to succeed President Hayes, we will notify our readers by telephone.

We have now placed the reader in possession of all the facts worth knowing in connection with the history of America from its very earliest discovery up to ten o'clock last night; but before finally releasing his button-hole we beg to "show him round" a little among our peculiar institutions, and call his attention to a few evidences of national greatness which may never have struck him before.

Let us, then, turn over a new leaf and open a new chapter.

CHAPTER XXVI.

PROGRESS.

OUR PATENT OFFICE REPORT—IS NECESSITY THE MOTHER OF INVENTION?—A CASE IN CONTRADICTION—ELECTRICAL KITE—THE COTTON GIN—THE FIRST RAILWAY TRAIN—THE FIRST STEAMBOAT—THE PRINTING PRESS—THE ATLANTIC CABLE—MORMONISM—AN APPARATUS—ART MATTERS.

Popular superstition has it that necessity is the mother of invention. We are sorry to deprive the world of an old saying, but we happen to know a person to whom the world is indebted for more useful inventions than any other person of our acquaint-

FRANKLIN AND HIS KITE

ance, and her name is Accident. For instance,

ELECTRICITY

was accidentally discovered by that famous American statesman and philosopher, Benjamin Franklin, while indulging in his favorite pastime of flying a kite. He ascertained that it was unsafe to fly a kite in a thunder storm unless you have a lightning rod attached to your spinal column. This important discovery conferred upon society the priceless boon of the lightning-rod man.

THE COTTON GIN

is an American invention, but whether it compares favorably with "Old Tom" or "London Dock" we are unable to say. We do not believe in stimulants as a rule, yet it cannot be denied that the introduction of

COTTON GIN.

the new-fangled gin greatly stimulated the cultivation of cotton in America.

THE FIRST RAILWAY TRAIN.

America took the lead in railroad construction, though the locomotive is claimed as an English contrivance.

The first railway train was a somewhat crude affair, but it succeeded in making a sensation. The locomotive was built by Peter Cooper, and he it was who ran the machine on its experimental trip.

The passengers were a surgeon, a chaplain, an editor, (names forgotton,) John Smith, and another fellow, (all dead-heads.) Mr. Cooper poked the fire, the other fellow pushed behind, while John Smith urbanely acted as cow-catcher. The clergyman rode in the smoking-car and meditated on the

THE FIRST RAILWAY TRAIN.

probabilities of ever seeing his family again this side of Jordan. The editor went to sleep, while the doctor sat behind ready to jump out and save himself in case of accident.

After a delightful excursion of fifty miles or so into the country the party returned home—afoot.

THE FIRST STEAMBOAT

was discovered by Robert Fulton September 4th, 1807. Our special artist was promptly on the spot, and we are thus enabled to lay before our readers all that is worth knowing of this event in the picture opposite.

THE TEN-CYLINDER PRINTING PRESS.

Newspapers have become a household necessity in every well-regulated American

THE FIRST STEAMBOAT—FASTEST TIME ON RECORD.

family. They mould public opinion, and are handy to light fires with. The universal use of newspapers gave rise to the ten-cylinder printing press, an American invention.

The publication of a daily newspaper is one of the most lucrative professions of the day, and we strongly advise our American youth to abandon all idea of ever becoming President, and save up all their pennies to start newspapers with when they grow up. An ably-conducted daily newspaper brings from two and a half to three cents per pound at the junk dealers, when times are good. On page 193 are some illustrated features of a well-conducted newspaper office. The central picture is full of tender pathos. The editor and proprietor (evidently a man of slender

PASTE
PORTRAIT OF THE EDITOR.
DAILY PUFF
THE PRESS ROOM.
BUSINESS DEPARTMENT.
FIGHTING EDITOR.

means) is seen working off his edition, assisted by his near relatives. Each individual, from the proud wife and doting mother to the infant at her breast, seems to attach weight to the enterprise with a degree of enthusiasm that ought to encourage any man.

THE ATLANTIC CABLE.

The Electro-Magnetic Submarine Trans-Atlantic Anglo-American Telegraph Cable is, perhaps, the most wonderful of all Yankee notions. By its agency our great morning dailies are able to get the most unreliable foreign news at the low rate of ten dollars per word. The only wonder is how people on both sides of the water ever got on so long without the cable.

On page 195 is a picture representing the submarine cable, for which we cannot help

III
THE ATLANTIC CABLE

suspecting the artist has drawn largely on his imagination.

MORMONISM

is of doubtful origin. Some authorities give the credit of its invention to Joseph Smith, while others do not hesitate to ascribe its origin to a gentlemen whom the mind naturally associates with sulphuric gases. However that may be, Mormonism is one of the institutions of the country, and Brigham Young is its prophet, his present address being Salt Lake City, Utah.

Mr. Young makes a specialty of matrimony, and has taken strict precautions to guard against widowhood, as will be seen by reference to our illustration, in which are seen Mr. and Mrs. Young on their bridal tour.

B.Y.
MR. AND MRS.
BRIGHAM
YOUNG.

Brigham makes it a point of etiquette to marry every unmarried lady to whom he happens to be introduced, and his life is a perennial honeymoon. To the merely Gentile man, whose matrimonial experience has been conducted on monogamic principles, the hardihood of Mr. Young is simply appalling.

AN APPARATUS

to keep hens from setting is an effervescence of the fertile brain of, well, no matter who. It speaks for itself.

For further information on the interesting subject of Yankee ingenuity we commend the reader's careful perusal of the United States Patent Office Report, a work unequaled for the brilliancy of its conception and startling dramatic situa-

AN INGENIOUS INVENTION.

tions, and which, for its conscientious adhesion to facts, only has a rival in the present work.

ART MATTERS.

The visitor to the Capitol, at Washington, will be struck with the paucity of American art, as evinced by the specimens of painting and sculpture to be seen in the Rotunda and immediate vicinity of that structure. Barrels of paint and whole quarries of marble have been sacrificed by an inscrutable Congress, whose sole object seems to have been to frighten its constituency away from the scene of its dark plottings with grotesque Washingtons, fantastic Lincolns, thinly-clad Indian ladies, and unprincipled looking Puritans. Some meritorious works of art, however, have lately found their way to the Capitol by accident, but let us have more of them. We humbly submit a few designs for equestrian statuary, which only await a misappropriation by Congress, as follows :

PLATE I.—Statue for a great American military hero who always kept his face to the foe.

EQUESTRIAN STATUARY.

PLATE II.—Is for another great military hero (a member of militia) who would have kept his face to the foe if circumstances had been favorable.

EQUESTRIAN STATUARY.

PLATE III.—Equestrian statue of a public gentleman who kept his face wherever it suited his convenience.

EQUESTRIAN STATUARY.

PLATE IV.--A statue (also equestrian) for a great politician of foreign origin who rose from humble beginnings to great achievements.

CHAPTER XXVII.

SOME ABORIGINAL IDEAS—WISE MEN AT WORK—MOUND BUILDING FROM FORCE OF HABIT—SUBTERRANEAN MISCELLANY—THE LOST TRIBE THEORY WON'T DO—AUTOGRAPH SPECIMEN OF PICTURE WRITING—LIGHT AT LAST—PICTURESQUE HABITS OF THE INDIANS.

The origin of the North American Indian has always been shrouded in the deepest mystery, and wise-heads of every age and clime have sought to tear aside the veil and show us our aboriginal brother in his true colors.

Some of these learned gentlemen have carried their zeal to the extent of renting wigwams in the Indian country, and living among these primitive children of the forest, hoping, by dint of listening at key-holes, to overhear some remark dropped by them that would reveal where they emigrated from, but nothing came of it but premature baldness to the wise-head so investigating. Others again have comfortably settled down into the belief that these singular members of society are a revised edition of the strayed or stolen tribes of Israel that have so long been advertised for in vain.

In support of this theory the latter class of philosophers has dived into side hills, (supposed to have been thrown up by an eccentric race of Indians known as mound builders,) turning up every conceivable article of second-hand Indian miscellany, and asking the world to believe that these mysterious "mounds" were simply subterraneous pawnbroker's shops, built and conducted in obedience to a well-known national instinct, and that the articles they contain are nothing more nor less than unredeemed pledges "left" by impecunious prehistoric ladies and gentlemen who were compelled to resort to that means of raising the wind.

On page 209 our artist shows us the exponents of the latter theory at work, and also gives us a singularly correct drawing of some of the bric-a-brac which they have unearthed. We will take the liberty of explaining further, and tell all we know concerning the supposed uses of these mysterious articles.

A is supposed to be a surgical instrument. B, an instrument of torture. C, toilet article. D, lady's ear ornament. E,

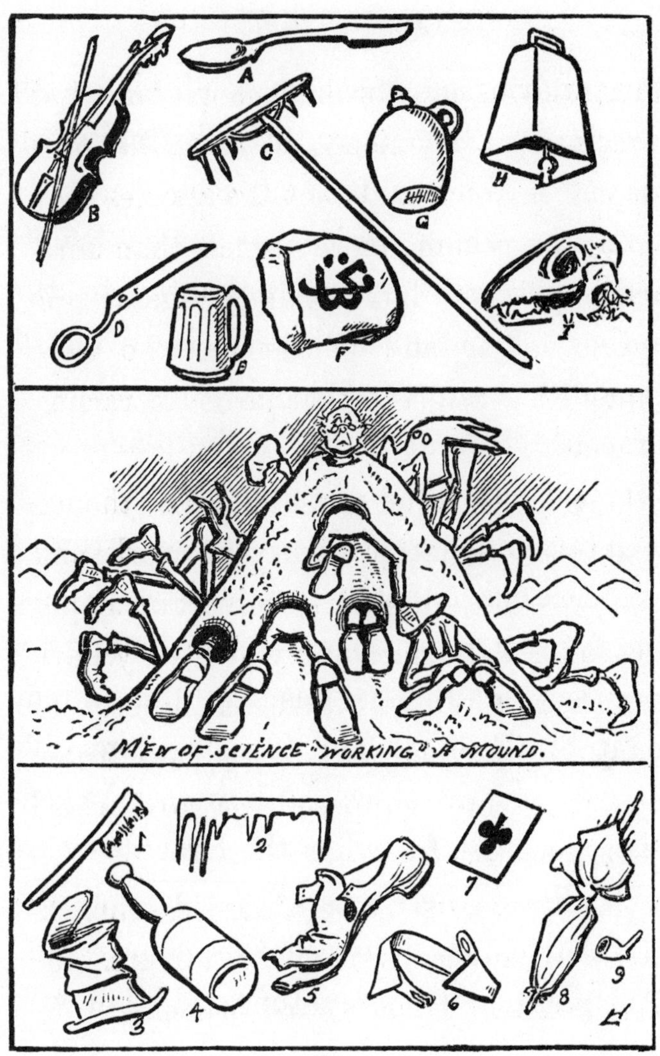
A
B
C
G
H
D
E
F
I
MEN OF SCIENCE "WORKING" A MOUND.
1
2
7
3
4
5
6
8
9

ancient drinking vessel. F, tombstone, with inscription. G, pottery. H, musical instrument. I, skull of native (deceased).

In the lower series we have: No. 1, artist's utensil. 2, uses unknown to the author. 3, patent hen's nest (badly out of repair). 4, vinaigrette. 5, projectile. 6, bracelet. 7, war club. 8, burglar's tool (very ancient). 9, cooking utensil.

After going carefully over this array of evidence one naturally hesitates before looking further for a theory. But, taking for granted that the Indians really are a remnant of those mislaid Israelites, the difficulty next arises as to how the dickens they got here, for when the Israelites were first missed there was as yet no railway communication between this country and Asia, and unless they tunneled their way up through, *via* China, it is difficult to account for their presence here.

In common with other great minds, we, too, have devoted much of our spare time to the effort of setting our red brother on his legs before the world, and of tracing his footprints back through the ages, but until quite recently we have been uniformly baffled. The fact is, our red brother ought really to have kept a diary. He would thus have saved us wise-acres much trouble and unnecessary expense. The next time we hope he will not overlook this important detail.

As we said, all our efforts to trace the Indians back to their origin had failed until recently. We rejected the "remnant" theory after a fair trial. We compared this remnant with the original piece (so claimed), and found it a bad match. In the face of strong evidence we renewed our efforts, which were destined to meet with reward, as will be seen presently.

A month or two since it luckily occurred to us to address a letter to a skillful sachem, (who happens to be an acquaintance of ours, and is at present located out West,) upon this interesting subject.

This gentleman, who is of the Choctaw persuasion, and was christened *Gimmechawtybackee*, (*Billious Jake*,) sent us a most courteous and comprehensive reply, which came to hand a few days since, and which covers the whole ground in the most lucid manner. We wonder we never thought of it before.

We here insert *Billious Jake's* letter

THE SACHEM'S LETTER.

TUPPER
CIGARS
1
2
3
4
U.P.R.R. Co

verbatim. It is a master-piece of composition, and sets the matter forever at rest. (*Daily papers please copy.*)

Before changing the subject, we should really like to pictorially look into the habits of these strange victims of circumstances. Examine page 214, if you please. In No. 1 we see a stony-hearted savage taking a very mean advantage of a white captive, and torturing him to death in the most horrible and deliberate manner. No. 2, an early settler pursued by a native. No. 3, Indian barber. And lastly, in No. 4, we have an Indian gentleman journeying towards the setting sun on dead-head principles.

"His faithful dog shall bear him company."—CAMPBELL.

CHAPTER XXIX.

SOME WORD PAINTING ON THE SUBJECT OF THE AMERICAN EAGLE—THE AFFAIRS OF THIS STRANGE EVENTFUL HISTORY WOUND UP.

A work of this nature would be incomplete without some slight allusion to the American Eagle. With reference to that ornithological specimen, we may remark that the first century of his career has been an eventful one. His wings have from time to time been cropped by foreign foes in a style that has made it unnecessary as well as impossible to scorch them against the sun. His tail feathers have been extracted by internecine strife in a manner

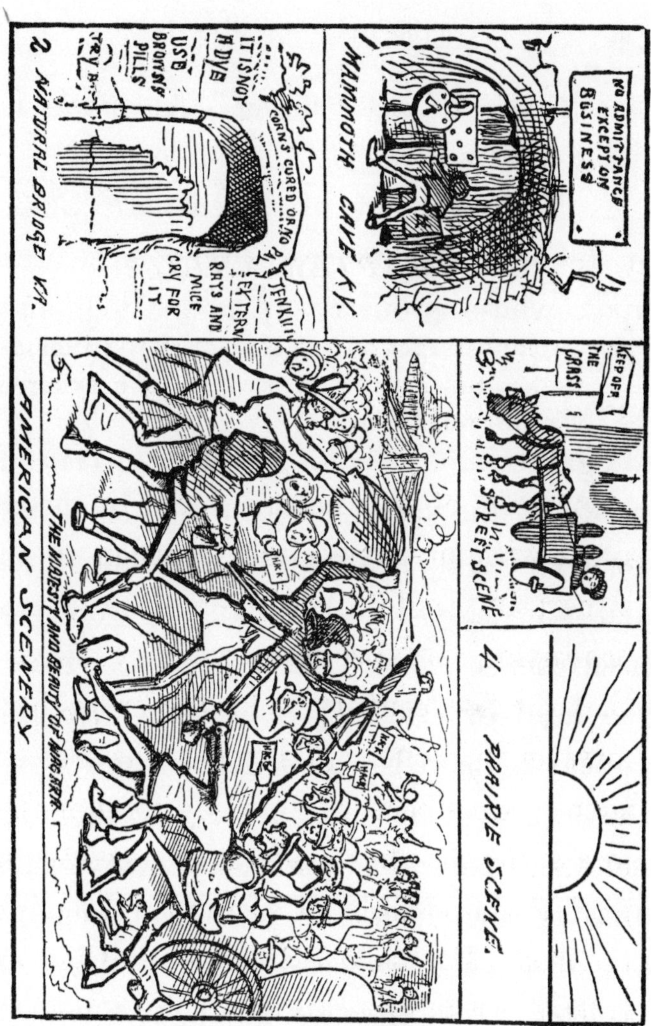
NO ADMITTANCE EXCEPT ON BUSINESS
MAMMOTH CAVE KY.
KEEP OFF THE GRASS
3 STREET SCENE
4 PRAIRIE SCENE.
CORNS CURED OR NO PAY
IT IS NOT A DYE
USE BROWN'S PILLS
RATS AND MICE CRY FOR IT
HACK
2 NATURAL BRIDGE VA.
5 THE MAJESTY AND BEAUTY OF NIAGARA
AMERICAN SCENERY

which the tourist "doing" American is liable at any moment to stumble upon.

In No. 1 we have the Mammoth Cave. It takes its name from the gentleman upon whose property it is located, and who uses it as a sub-cellar in Winter, and locks himself up in it during the tax-gathering season. Our illustration treats of the latter period. The Natural Bridge (No. 2) is a marvel of architecture, and is lavishly decorated with appropriate inscriptions. No. 3 hardly comes under the head of *Natural Scenery*, and would appear to be rather a sudden change from the sweet realms of nature to the busy haunts of men; but contrast is everything, and we turn from this turbulent scene to one of delicious repose. No. 4, a Western prairie. Here the eye wanders off over a rich and varied landscape of level country, till finally in the distance it encounters what? a vast spider? No. That is only the setting sun, as we ascertained in a private conversation with the artist. No. 5. We hardly know how to treat this matter. In writing about Niagara it is customary to either rush madly into poetry or break hysterically into exclamation points. We had heard a great deal about the awful majesty of Niagara Falls, and went there to obtain, if possible, a personal interview, intending to write it up in a style that would bankrupt our printer. We say we went there expecting much, but we found that the half had not been told us. If it had, we should have remained at home. Perhaps the least said about it the better.

CHAPTER XXVIII.

AMERICAN SCENERY.

Few countries can boast such a variety of natural features as our own America.

To the intelligent tourist of unlimited bank account this country affords abundant material for the study of nature with all the modern improvements, including gas, hot and cold water, and an elevator running every five minutes up to the fifteenth floor. Terms invariably in advance.

Our illustration on the opposite page conveys but a feeble idea of the magnitude of some of the wonderful freaks of nature

PORTRAIT OF THE AMERICAN EAGLE.

that has made it extremly difficult for him to steer his majestic course amid the blue ether of Freedom, and his flight at times has been awkward and eccentric in the extreme. In short, the plumage has been plucked from various parts of his body by divers evil-disposed persons to such an extent as to make aerial navigation in a rarefied atmosphere an uncomfortable, not to say highly injurious pursuit.

Notwithstanding all this we feel authorized to inform the public that our national fowl is as tough as a boarding-house spring chicken; that he will continue to roost at his present address until further notice, spreading his wings from the Atlantic to the Pacific, beneath the shadow of which all persons of good character are invited to come (references exchanged). Here every one, from the peon to the prince, if not satisfied with his present situation, can find a refuge, and by strict attention to business become an Alderman of somebody else's native village and have canal boats named after him, or, (by *very* strict attention to business) even rise to be President* of the United States!

THE END.

---

*NOTE—Since the above piece of rhetoric went to press we have ascertained (quite accidentally) that persons are not eligible to this office who have the misfortune to be born abroad. Therefore we hastily append this postscript lest any unsuspecting peon or prince who might chance to read these pages be inveigled over here under a misapprehension. If he comes now it must be on his own responsibility.